Catherine's Remembrance

LATTER-DAY DAUGHTERS

BOOKS IN THE LATTER-DAY DAUGHTERS SERIES

1832 Maren's Hope
1838 Laurel's Flight
1840 Hannah's Treasure
1844 Anna's Gift
1846 Catherine's Remembrance
1856 Clarissa's Crossing
1862 Violet's Garden
1896 Esther's Celebration
1897 Ellie's Gold
1910 Sarah's Quest
1918 Gracie's Angel
1978 Marciea's Melody

Catherine's Remembrance

LATTER-DAY DAUGHTERS

Carol Lynch Williams

Published by
Deseret Book Company
Salt Lake City, Utah

*To those who traveled the unmarked road
so we could safely dwell here*

© 1997 Carol Lynch Williams

All rights reserved. No part of this book may be reproduced in any form or by any means without permission in writing from the publisher, Deseret Book Company, P. O. Box 30178, Salt Lake City, Utah 84130. This work is not an official publication of The Church of Jesus Christ of Latter-day Saints. The views expressed herein are the responsibility of the author and do not necessarily represent the position of the Church or of Deseret Book Company.

Deseret Book and Cinnamon Tree are registered trademarks of Deseret Book Company.

Library of Congress Cataloging-in-Publication Data
Williams, Carol Lynch.
   Catherine's remembrance / by Carol Lynch Williams.
      p.   cm. — (The Latter-day Daughters series)
   Summary: In 1846, when religious persecution forces her family to leave Illinois and flee west to find a new home, twelve-year-old Catherine finds herself questioning her parents' Mormon faith, until she discovers a bundle of old letters written by her mother years earlier.
   ISBN 1-57345-296-3 (pbk.)
   [1. Mormons—Fiction. 2. Frontier and pioneer life—Fiction. 3. Mothers and daughters—Fiction.] I. Title. II. Series.
PZ7.W65588Cat   1997
[Fic]—dc21   97-30548
                                                                          CIP
                                                                          AC

Printed in the United States of America   8006-4589
10   9   8   7   6   5   4   3   2

Contents

Chapter 1
Worries 1

Chapter 2
Talking with Pa 10

Chapter 3
Time with Ma 21

Chapter 4
Learning 33

Chapter 5
Brigham Young 43

Chapter 6
Almost Time 52

Chapter 7
Learning for Myself 64

Chapter 8
My Own Remembrance 74

Glossary 83

What Really Happened 87

CHAPTER ONE

Worries

"I don't wanna go," I said to Ma, running lots of little steps to match the long strides she took.

Ma ignored me, looking neither to the right nor the left, just walking hard to the wagon that she and Pa were filling up with our belongings.

"I hate this moving," I said. "I been moving all my life and I hate it."

Ma handed piles of blankets up to Pa.

"That child still running on,* Olive?" Pa asked.

"She is." Ma grinned full in my face, showing her pretty white teeth. Her look made me smile,

---

See the glossary at the end of this book for an explanation of unusual words and expressions marked with an asterisk (*).

too, though I had decided at the start I wasn't going to smile this whole trip. I turned quick so no one could see that Ma's grin had made one of my own twitch across my face.

"Got something for me, girl?" Pa asked.

"Yes, sir," I said, and handed Pa a small box of Ma's most precious things: her remembrances. "Ma said you're to put that in a place where it'll be safe."

Pa leaned out the back of the wagon and took the box from me. "Did she, now?"

"Yes, sir." I looked Pa right in the eye. His eyes were dark, so dark that sometimes people thought them black. But I could see the brown, because I saw that same color in my own eyes when I looked in Ma's reflecting glass.

"And where's *your* box?" Pa balanced the carved wooden case on one hip, then, scooping up the blankets, straightened up tall.

"There's no room for it," I said.

Brother Brigham had told families to take all they could. The place we were headed, wherever that might be, wouldn't have shops to buy new items. We needed to go prepared. But children's things weren't that important. My collections would have to stay behind.

"No room for the box like your Ma's? Are you saying we should break up a pair?"

"Pa, you told me we could only take what we needed. You said yourself that we'd bring nothing friv'lous."*

"We're building a new world, Catherine. There won't be anything waiting for us when we arrive. I'm sure I can find a place for that box, seeing that it means so much to you."

"Oh, Pa," I said. "You know it does." Another smile started across my face. I turned before he could see it.

"Run then," Pa said.

I met Ma in the doorway, carrying out the last of the supplies. Ma worked hard, even though she was in the family way.* Nothing could slow her down, not even Pa telling her to take it easy.

"Make sure your room is neat, Catherine," she said as she passed.

"Yes ma'am," I said. But I thought, *Why, Ma? Won't be anybody living in this place but somebody who doesn't like Mormons.*

Catherine's Remembrance

I went to the parlor where many of our belongings remained unpacked. The wagon could only hold so much. Even though we were going to start a brand new city in a part of the country far from the rest of the Americans, we couldn't take everything. There just wasn't room.

I looked at the fancy things Ma had begun collecting since our move from Kirtland. As soon as Brother Joseph had said Nauvoo would be our Zion, Ma had begun to make this house our home. It bothered me. Ill feelings crawled around under my skin like ants on a dead grasshopper.

"It sure isn't right," I said, low. "I don't see why they can drive us out again. I don't see why Ma and Pa keep following these people from place to place."

I looked around quick to see if anyone had heard my words. No, Ma and Pa were still out at the wagon.

"I don't wanna go," I told the parlor. "I think I should be able to stay right here, if I want."

I wondered how many people would stay behind. Would everyone follow Brother Brigham out west?

Catherine's Remembrance

I went to the bookcase Pa had made from a Mississippi oak tree. That's where I had hidden my box, at the back of the bottom shelf. It wasn't really hidden. Whoever took over our place would have found it right away. And it would have meant nothing to them except maybe a bit of something to burn in the fireplace.

I knelt on the floor, smoothing my brown gingham dress around me. Reaching into the deep shelf, I pulled out my box and opened it. A few feathers lay colorful on the golden tan of the wood.

Ma's box was full of important remembrances. Would mine ever have anything more in it than feathers?

I closed the lid. I needed a remembrance of this place, I decided.

Ma was inside now. I could hear her voice, echoing in the bedroom above as she called out the window to Pa.

"Tomorrow will be a beautiful day, Michael," she said.

"How can she be excited?" I said out loud. I

felt angry inside. "Why does she want to leave again?"

"She's following God, Catherine," Pa said.

I whirled around, still on my knees. "Pa," I said.

Aunt Millie, Ma's sister, stood nearby. She looked irritated.

Pa came and knelt before me, getting right down close to my face, so close I could smell his breath. It was oniony from dinner. I lowered my head, but Pa lifted my chin with his finger. His rough hand was gentle on my skin. I looked into his eyes.

"Don't you know it yet?" Pa asked. "Your ma and I are following what our Father in Heaven has asked us to do. Don't you believe?"

Now I couldn't look my pa in the eye, so I stared down into my box. I stared at the feathers.

"It's not fair," I began.

"Following God isn't fair?"

"I want to be here," I said. "I want to stay in Nauvoo."

Aunt Millie *tsk*ed. Aunt Millie is always *tsk*ing at things I say. I acted as if she wasn't standing in my front room and kept on talking. "I want us to have a home. I want you and me and Ma to be someplace for more than a few years," I said.

"Michael," Aunt Millie said. "Rein in your child. She speaks too much for a twelve-year-old."

Pa looked back over his shoulder at the heavyset woman. "We've always wanted to know Catherine's thoughts."

"Children should be seen and not heard."

"In some homes," Pa said.

Ma came into the parlor then. "Millie, care for a warm drink on such a cool evening?"

Aunt Millie waited a second, then started after Ma into the kitchen. "Spare the rod, spoil the child," she said, loud enough that I could hear.

"Busybody," I said.

"Don't judge," Pa said. I knew he was ready to listen. "Tell me your thoughts."

"I want to stay in one place, Pa. You know that. I don't want to go anywhere. I'm scared to."

Pa folded his long legs under himself and sat down. "There's nothing to feel scared about," he said.

I leaned forward. "There's plenty," I said. "I

heard people talking about the rivers we have to cross. And about the mountains. And, Pa, we're not even sure where we're going to."

"Brother Brigham knows where we're going," Pa said. "To stay in Nauvoo would mean the death of us all, starting with Brigham Young. There are men trying to have him arrested."

"But it's so cold now. I thought we were going to wait till summer to leave."

"That was the promise the governor made to Brother Brigham. We *were* supposed to wait. But they're trying to get into Nauvoo by the back door. I'll be surprised if we get even one red cent for our property. Catherine, it's not safe here anymore."

I looked hard at Pa and then searched inside myself. "I'm afraid. I'm not sure why."

Pa leaned close to me and kissed my forehead. His lips were dry. "I'll keep you safe. And if we rely on the Lord, all will be well." He stood then and started back to finish the packing. "We're leaving at first light on the morrow.* There's still things to be done here. Hurry that box out to me." And he was gone.

Catherine's Remembrance

I sat still a moment more.

There was much to be afraid of: the rivers to cross, Ma's baby coming when we were on the trail to our new Zion, leaving so much behind, Indians. But mostly I was afraid of the feeling that had been wearing at me for a long time now.

I wasn't sure God really *did* want us to go out west. I wasn't sure if I even believed the way my ma and pa did.

CHAPTER TWO

Talking with Pa

I wandered upstairs to my bedroom to see what remembrance I could find to take with me.

My clothes press* was empty. My bed was bare of its mattress. Only the ropes that had sup-

ported it were left, tied crisscross to the wooden frame. Pa thought he'd be able to make me a new bed once we built our home. But the goose-down mattress had

taken Ma a long time to save for. It was packed in the wagon already with our few other things, waiting to leave.

Under my window, on a long, low table that Pa had built especially for me, was my collection. Lined in neat rows, according to size, were the pretty stones I had been saving for years. I hadn't found them all myself. Sometimes family members gave me things that they found. I had stones that looked pretty enough to be diamonds. And different colors, too. It was like a little rainbow on my table: pink, blue, yellow, green, purple.

There was shiny black rock, a tiny bit of gold somebody had given me from North Carolina, some silver, and even a few arrowheads.

Once Uncle Ford had brought me an ugly round rock. "Crack it open, Catherine."

Pa and I did, and there in the center of it was what looked like a tiny diamond mine, shiny and beautiful.*

But rocks were too heavy to take. We were carrying other precious things: flour, sugar, seeds, a tent that Ma had helped make, and a few slips* from the fruit trees in our yard so we could plant them later. Our mattresses were packed away, along with blankets, things to cook with, and a piece of pretty stained glass window Ma wanted to put in our new home.

"We don't even know where we're going," I said to myself.

Pa believed we did. He said Brother Brigham had sent scouts ahead, that our leader had been studying maps of the West for a long time.

But how was I to know any of that? I hadn't seen the maps. I hadn't heard any scouts talking.

Angry, I looked around the room. "There is no remembrance of this place to take with me," I said at last, then I went outside into the cold.

I carried my box to Pa. I watched as he slid it 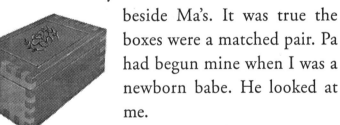 beside Ma's. It was true the boxes were a matched pair. Pa had begun mine when I was a newborn babe. He looked at me.

"I'm thinking on going inside and getting something to warm me up right now. Want to go in with me, Catherine?"

I looked past Pa at the sun fading in the distance. It was a cold February evening.

We should be settling down to reading, I

thought, *not getting ready to flee our homes.* But I said, "I don't think so, Pa. Aunt Millie, she makes me nervous. She's always looking to see that you and Ma correct me. She thinks I'm too light-minded."

"Are you, girl?" Pa stepped off the back of the wagon and it squeaked a bit. He came over to where I stood, wrapped up against the cold.

I thought a moment. "No, sir." I looked up at my pa. I believed him to be the bravest and smartest man in the world. He had graduated from college. He held fast to the ideas of thinking and speaking free, which was the very reason I was allowed to tell him and Ma my thoughts on things. "No, sir. I'm not light-minded. I'm a wonder-er."

Pa nodded. "I knew you would be." He put his arm out to me like I was a real lady. I took his crooked elbow and we started into the house. "We'll speak in the parlor until Aunt Millie has gone. I'll tell you a memory of mine. One that I hold dear. Then we'll get something to warm us."

"Yes, sir."

We went inside. The fire in the parlor did

little to warm the room, probably because it was so cold outside and we had been opening and closing the doors so much in our hurry to pack.

Pa sat on the sofa and I snuggled up near him. In the kitchen I could hear Ma talking with Aunt Millie. Ma's voice was soft, and I couldn't make out what she was saying. But Aunt Millie's voice came out loud, and words like *cold, wagons,* and *Brother Brigham* slipped in to Pa and me.

I turned off my ears to the other room and looked at Pa, waiting.

"Catherine, the moment you were born," Pa said, "I knew you'd be exactly like your ma. That's why I made you two matching boxes." He looked toward the kitchen and I followed his gaze.

Aunt Millie's voice boomed out like cannon fire. "The river's unsafe at this time of year."

Ma's soothing voice came toward me, the words unclear, and I closed my eyes against the thought of crossing the great river.

My hands tightened in my lap. The Mississippi *was* unsafe. Why, ice floated through it. How would we ever cross?

"Catherine?"

Catherine's Remembrance

"Yes, sir?"

"I'm about to tell you a most amazing thing. I want you to know a little about your entrance into this world and into our family. I want you to know how it is that you remind me of your ma."

"I'm listening, Pa."

He started his story again. I listened hard to his words and pushed the picture of the icy Mississippi from my mind. I tried to think of New York almost thirteen years ago. Had May 31 been a warm day in 1833?

"Your cry filled our home," Pa said. "It bounced right off the ceiling and continued so long and strong I thought the dogs would start barking."

I smiled. "You mean, Pa, Ma is a boisterous woman?"

Pa laughed. "Far from that. Your ma is quiet and humble. But looking at you so little and loud and new, I knew that you'd be like your ma. Wanting to remember things. Wanting to always be learning. Wanting to be happy. So I made you both the boxes."

"How could you tell, Pa? How could you tell I'd be like Ma?"

"Just one of those feelings. One of those feelings burning in my heart. When you were born I couldn't remember ever feeling closer to heaven." Pa stared off at nothing and didn't speak for a minute. It was like he was back in time, watching the whole thing over again in his mind. *That's a pretty good remembrance,* I thought. But I couldn't put it in my box.

I wondered how it was that a screaming baby could make anyone feel close to heaven. It was another one of those things that Pa knew and I had no idea about. Would I ever have those kinds of feelings? Would I ever want to follow the leaders of this religion? Would I ever know the Church was where I was supposed to be the way Ma and Pa did?

Ma and Aunt Millie appeared at the doorway. Outside sleet rained up against the house.

"I'll be on my way," Aunt Millie said. "Ford'll be waiting on me. He's been packing up the wagon all this day since the announcement to leave."

Pa stood and walked over to Aunt Millie. Although she was Ma's sister, I couldn't see even a bit of resemblance between them as I sat looking at the two. Aunt Millie looked a million years older than Ma. Maybe that was what Millie was short for: million.

"Good-bye, Catherine," Aunt Millie said.

"Good-bye," I said, not quite meeting her eyes.

"Perhaps this trip west will change your spirit some, so that you'll show a bit more obedience to your elders."

I jumped to my feet, ready to spout out the anger that bubbled up inside me. Aunt Millie sure could do that to a soul, make them feel angry as God did at the time of Noah. Then I saw Ma and Pa's faces.

Ma wore a small smile. Her thick brown hair was coming loose a bit. It was wispy near her pale skin.

I closed my eyes for a moment and then, opening them, looked right at Aunt Millie and said, "I hope you sleep well, Auntie. I hope that Uncle Ford won't snore too loud this night."

CATHERINE'S REMEMBRANCE

Surprise moved across Aunt Millie's face. I hurried quick with what I was saying. "I only know that he snores because I heard you talking once at the Sunday meeting."

Aunt Millie's mouth dropped open. "Why, you were eavesdropping."

"No, ma'am. I was standing with a group of my friends. You were talking so loud everyone heard it. Some of the girls laughed, but not me. I've seen Uncle Ford napping in your front room. So, I do wish things get better with him. Maybe you have some herbs that would stop his snores."

Aunt Millie straightened her shoulders and started to say something, but I spoke again.

"And I hope, too, that those warts on your knees have dissolved to nothing. Maybe that poultice* worked."

Aunt Millie's mouth flapped. Then she turned on her heel and, without even a good-bye to Ma and Pa, left. When the door closed, my folks turned on me together.

"Catherine Olive Hansen," Ma said.

"What, Ma?" I asked. "I really did mean it in

the best of ways. Warts on your knees must be awful."

Ma *tsk*ed like Aunt Millie always does and started out of the room. I saw a hint of a smile.

"Catherine," Pa said, his face stern. "How'd you know that about the warts? Did you hear that at Sunday meeting also?"

"No, sir. It was at Aunt Millie's house."

"She invited you in to talk about such things?"

I bowed my head. "Ma sent me with a bit of lace to Aunt Millie's. She was sitting with some women, making a quilt. Everybody that day talked of her own ailments."

"Is that so? And you heard about these ailments while delivering something for your mother?"

"No, Pa," I said, again not meeting his eye. "I heard that whilst I was lingering. Outside under the window."

"Catherine, I've taught you better than to eavesdrop."

"Yes, sir, I know. But it was so interesting. I really didn't mean to listen, but my ears just had to hear."

Pa stood quiet a moment.

I looked at him. Now he wore a bit of a smile.

"Pa," I said, my voice low. "You want to know any more of the ailments? Aunt Millie's warty knees weren't the worst things."

Pa turned and as he left the room called back, "No, thank you, Catherine. The knees are enough for me."

CHAPTER THREE

Time with Ma

Ma woke me early the next morning. "Breakfast," she said, "then we leave. Your pa's gathering up the stock. He's taking a few of your favorite chickens."

I nodded from my pallet on the floor. It was so cold in my room I could see my breath.

"Come dress by the fire in the kitchen," Ma said. "You'll have time before Pa gets back in. Then you can fold these blankets and we can get them in the wagon."

I leapt to my feet and pulled my wool dress from a peg in the clothes press. I grabbed my shoes and stockings and ran through the cold rooms down to the kitchen. The air here was like a warm breath. The cookstove seemed to glow.

I dressed as quickly as I could, my chilly fingers fumbling with the buttonhook* as I did up my shoes.

"Go rebraid your hair in the parlor," Ma said. "I'll dish you up breakfast."

"Oh, Ma," I said. "It's so warm here."

Ma opened her mouth to say something, then shut it again. "You're right. And later it's going to be cold enough for you anyway. Stand far from the table then. The brush is over by the shelf."

"Thank you, Ma."

There was no looking glass* to work with, but I set to doing what Ma had asked in the far part of the room. I loosened my hair, letting it fall, heavy, down my back. It was so long now I could sit on it. I brushed fast. Strands floated ghostlike, following the brush with every stroke.

Ma watched me from across the room.

"My Catherine," she said. Her voice was soft.

"What, Ma?"

Catherine's Remembrance

Ma walked over to me. "I'll do your hair for you this morning. Come sit here."

Ma drew a chair along behind her. She placed it as far from the table as she could. I sat down and she began to brush my hair.

It had been a long time since Ma had done this for me.

"You're becoming a young woman, Catherine," she said.

"Hmmm," I said and wondered. Was that what I wanted to be, a young woman? Some of my girlfriends couldn't wait to marry. "No, thank you, Ma," I said. "I'll stay your daughter a while longer. I like being your friend."

Ma's hands felt gentle. "Why, Catherine Olive Hansen, you'll always be my daughter, no matter what happens. And my friend, too."

"I'd like to stay your daughter in your home, then."

"Are you thinking of marriage?" Ma's voice sounded surprised. We both knew of girls who, at fourteen, had gotten married.

"I only did briefly. Just long enough to know I didn't want to. Probably never, even."

Ma started braiding my hair. Her hands could nearly fly doing work such as this, but this morning she worked slow and careful.

"Perhaps I'll go to the university like Pa did."

"Not many women do that," Ma said.

"I'd like to study rocks. I'd like to add on to my collection," I said. It bothered me not to take any of my rocks with us on this trip.

"You can do whatever you'd like," Ma said. "But keep your mind open if ever a man like your pa shows up." She placed her hands on my shoulders and said, "You're done."

I sat still with Ma's hands on me. *Oh, Ma,* I thought. *I want to stay here in Nauvoo with you and Pa.* I stood and turned, then put my arms around Ma, trying not to squeeze her big middle.

"It'll be fine," Ma said, hugging me back. "All will be well."

"I'm so scared, Ma. I don't want to leave."

"I know." Our voices were whispers.

I heard Pa come into the house. He burst into the kitchen where Ma and I were. I started to move away from Ma, but she held me close. I looked back over my shoulder at Pa.

"Are you crying?" he asked.

I shook my head, but Ma laughed a sad little laugh.

Pa came over and put his long arms around us both.

A lump came up in my throat. I tried to swallow it down.

"All will be well," he said.

Ma laughed her small laugh again. "Why, Michael, that's what I said."

"Then it must be true," Pa said.

We stood a moment longer, the three of us, until my stomach called out for breakfast.

"I think it's time to eat," Pa said. And so we did.

I climbed into the back of our wagon, wrapping my cloak around me. Pa and Ma climbed up on the riding board,* and Pa started the four oxen off with a click of his tongue and a snap of his whip.

The wind was biting. By the time we got down to the river, I wondered if my nose was even on my face anymore. The hens and geese tied to the side of our wagon in pens cackled so much I had to climb up near Ma and Pa so I could know if I was even thinking.

A line of wagons was before us, and an even longer line came behind. A long trail wound its way down to the edge of the Mississippi.

One by one the wagons were tied to a flatboat or a barge. I searched out the front of the wagon.

"Which is the biggest boat, Pa?" I asked.

Pa had gotten out of the wagon and moved up next to the oxen.

"What?" The cold weather had turned Pa's cheeks and nose bright red. The wind made his eyes water.

"I want us to get the biggest boat we can," I said.

Ma looked back at me. I expected her to say "Don't be selfish, Catherine Hansen." But she didn't.

"Are you frightened still?" Ma's voice was so kind it made me want to climb up onto her lap.

"Yes, ma'am," I said.

"And cold, too?"

"Yes, ma'am."

"Come sit up next to me until it's our turn to cross."

I climbed on the seat and squished close as I could to Ma.

Pa walked back to the wagon. "The Mississippi is a mile wide here."

I looked at the fast-flowing river. "We'll be swept away. All the way out to the ocean."

Pa laughed. "Of course we won't. The Nauvoo Police* are manning the barges. They'll take us across safely. And I'll help on the oars, too. You won't be riding in the wagon, though. I want you to stand on the boat. If we do lose control . . ."

"Pa," I said. It was hard to keep my voice quiet. "You said all would be well."

"I believe that, Catherine," Pa said. "But we must also be wise."

Pa walked up to talk to Aunt Millie and Uncle Ford. They were in the wagon in front of us.

I closed my eyes and thought of home. Right now I'd be helping Ma with chores if we were still there. We'd be reading the Book of Mormon together.

I pulled my cloak tighter. If I were home I'd

be warm. And I wouldn't have a fearful feeling in the pit of my stomach, either.

"Whoa!"

The shout made me jerk my head up. My eyes opened wide.

"Oh no," Ma said.

I looked out at the river, to the flatboat in front of my aunt and uncle.

"Calm 'em down!" a man screamed to another who moved across the boat to the oxen that were tethered* tightly to a short lead.

The boat waggled a bit in the water as the oxen fought to break loose.

"Those poor animals," I said to Ma, standing up so I could see better. "They're afraid."

Ma nodded.

"Calm 'em down. Careful or we'll lose the lot!" came a shout.

The oxen jerked free of their tether and plunged over the side of the boat into the icy Mississippi. They were yoked together.* They fought for a moment, frantic, bobbing in the water.

"Get them out!" I screamed from beside Ma.

But it was too late. The oxen went under water again and didn't come back up.

Pa was at my side in an instant. Ahead of us Uncle Ford was guiding his oxen and wagon onto the craft.

"Now, Catherine," Pa said, patting my arm.

"Pa," I said. "This is what I'm afraid of. Our oxen. And what about the milk cows and the sheep? What if they're swept overboard? What if our wagon topples over?"

"It won't happen," Pa said.

"How can you be sure? I can't swim too good, Pa. Especially not in cold water."

Ma put her arm around me and pulled me close. I glanced over at her. Her eyes were wide. I could tell by looking at her that she was worried, too.

"You won't need to know how to swim. I won't let you get into the water."

"How do you know that, Pa? How can you be so sure?"

"The knowledge is my heart, Catherine. I'm calm here." Pa pointed near his chest. "I know right here. Olive," Pa reached across me to Ma.

"Do you trust me? Do you have faith in the Lord?" he asked her.

"You know the answer to both those questions, Michael," Ma said.

Pa pulled Ma's hand to his lips and gave her a kiss.

We waited together until it was our turn.

"Climb on down," Pa said and he handed me and Ma to the ground. There was dirty snow piled up where we stood. The ground was muddy and lined with wagon tracks that slowly filled with water.

Pa helped the oxen pull the wagon onto the barge, then he unhooked them and tied them with a short rope to the barge bottom. I went back to help Ma lead the other animals on with us.

The wagon was lashed down* so it wouldn't move. The wheels were locked with a long stick. The rest of our animals were tied so they wouldn't bolt as the oxen on the boat before us had. Ma and I walked onto the barge last. I clutched at her hand.

Some of the water near the shore was frozen.

"Look, Ma," I said, pointing out into the deeper, fast-moving part of the river.

Large chunks of ice rode the waves of the Mississippi.

Our barge moved out further from the shore, caught the current, and swung out wide.

I screamed without meaning to.

Pa and the Nauvoo Police worked quickly, paddling and pushing the craft toward the far bank. The oxen began to lunge on the tethers. The chickens set up to squawking. The geese honked. The cows looked around wide-eyed and mooed in fear. The sound of the water seemed to rage in my ears.

"Oh, no, Ma!" I said. I pointed at a chunk of ice that moved from upriver. "It's going to hit us!"

The ice crashed into the side of the barge, making a loud thud.

We're going to break apart, I thought. But I couldn't make my mouth say the words.

More ice banged into the boat. Ma gulped in a great breath of air and pulled me close to her.

"Ma! Ma!" I cried. I knew how the oxen had

felt. I wanted to leap off the barge and swim for shore.

Ma's grip tightened. She leaned her mouth toward my ear and began to hum my favorite song, "A Mighty Fortress Is Our God."

A bit of peace entered my heart then. I was still afraid, so much that I kept my eyes closed while the ruckus was going on. But over the sounds of crashing ice, the chickens and sheep, the cows, oxen, and geese, and Pa and the Nauvoo Police calling to each other, Ma's voice rose and calmed me.

At last we reached the other side of the river. How long had it taken us? An hour? All day? A year?

Ma squeezed me up tight to her.

"My, Catherine," she said. "That was the longest mile I have ever experienced."

I had to agree with her.

CHAPTER FOUR

Learning

It was far past noon when we reached the opposite shore. I felt so eager to get off the river that I didn't think we'd ever dock so our wagon could be pulled off. I was glad I wouldn't be making the trip back and forth like these Nauvoo Police were doing.

Ma walked up to a man I could remember seeing in town but whose name I didn't know.

"Thank you for taking us safely across," she said.

"You're welcome, ma'am." He tipped his hat at Ma. He was young, and I wondered if all his ferryings would be like ours.

"You've a lot of work still to be done." Ma glanced across the river, where a long, white rope of covered wagons waited. "May the Lord help you and keep you safe."

Again the man tipped his hat to Ma. "Thank you, ma'am."

Pa hitched the oxen to our wagon. He drove up to the shore a bit, trying to get out of the mud near the shoreline. He walked back to where Ma and I stood close together to get warm.

"Madam," Pa said, bowing from the waist to Ma and then reaching out for her.

"Sir," Ma said, smiling.

He pulled her close, there on the shore in front of everyone. I looked around. Was anyone watching my parents now? No one seemed to even notice we were here. How could they, with a river still to cross?

"I told you we'd make it. Catherine, if you have faith, the Lord will guide you."

I nodded my head. How did Pa know for sure? How did Ma?

We walked over to the wagon and Pa helped Ma and me get in. Then he climbed up beside Ma and clicked to the oxen.* We started, following the tracks that rolled off before us. Not too far ahead, I could see Aunt Millie and Uncle Ford's wagon.

The sun looked cold. It sat high in the sky and seemed to be there only for light.

"Olive," Pa said. "I'm hungry. The wait and then the ride over took every bit of energy that I have. Is there something to eat that won't take much to fix? I don't want to stop unless we have to. I'd like to keep up with everyone else."

"Of course, Michael." Ma pointed to a basket near where I sat. "Catherine, can you bring that up to me?"

"Yes, Ma."

The wagon swung this way and that, bouncing over the rough spots in the trail. I crawled to the basket, rocking back and forth. There wasn't a lot of room, because Ma and Pa had packed so much to start our new lives with. I passed the basket to Ma over the top of a bag of flour.

We ate our noon meal late and on the road. But never had cold biscuits and cold stew tasted so good. I guess my fright had made me all the more hungry.

The swaying of the wagon might have put me

to sleep, but every bump and rock we hit, I felt. I moved this way and that, trying to get comfortable.

"Pa, do you think I might walk some?" I asked. I was sure we had been riding along for hours, and yet the sun held its place high in the sky.

"You could try, if you want. Stay right behind the cows. And call if we move too fast."

I dropped to the ground and ran back behind our two milk cows. They looked at me with their large, brown eyes. It didn't seem that they remembered crossing the river.

Pa started again.

I tramped along behind, stepping around mud holes, piles of dirty snow, and other reminders left by animals along the trail.

A brisk wind blew. My hands became numb. My lips would barely move. They felt frozen. So did my nose.

The oxen continued to plod along. They were so slow that I couldn't even warm up. *Which is worse?* I complained to myself. *Being knocked around in an uncomfortable wagon? Or walking behind cows in this terrible weather?* I decided things had to change.

"Pa," I called, after a long while. "I want to ride again."

"Catherine," Pa said, pulling the oxen to a halt. "In or out. Not both. I can't keep holding things up because you can't decide what to do."

"Yes, sir," I said.

Pa held out his hand for me. I grabbed hold and he pulled me up. I stepped over him and back into the wagon bed.

I sat down and the jostling began again.

I watched out the small hole in the back of the canvas that was the wagon cover.* The ground was snow-covered. The trees were bare of their leaves. Behind us came another family. Were they warmer than  we were? A soft rain fell. I could see my breath. After awhile I quit watching the road. It passed too slowly to interest me anymore. I crawled back into the wagon and tucked myself among our belongings.

It seemed we were moving along slower than a snail. I wondered if we would ever stop.

Ma looked back at me. "I brought things to read, Catherine. Would you like one?"

"Oh, yes, Ma."

"Most of my books are packed. But here are some old papers I've saved, *The Morning and Evening Star.* You could read through this and maybe a few of your questions would be answered. Many of the Prophet's words were written here."

I took a handful of the newsprint* from Ma. How had she known that I wondered about the gospel? Would the answers to my questions be found in the words that Joseph Smith said were commandments from God?

"Thank you," I said, and I settled back again, this time to read.

It was nine miles to the Sugar Creek camp where the Saints were gathering. But time passed faster once I started to read.

When I finally set the papers aside, my eyes tired from reading so long, I peered out through the opening in the canvas. The sky was beginning to take on a look of evening. A few hours ago, Ma had moved off the seat with Pa and come back with me. The ride in the wagon bed wasn't that much more comfortable. It was cramped for sure. But it sheltered us from the wind, at least. I felt bad for Pa, driving us along in the near-freezing weather. I was glad he had a warm coat and gloves and dry boots. A lot of people back in Nauvoo were not this well prepared.

I peered through the dim light at Ma. At first, I thought she was asleep. Her eyes were closed, the lashes dark on her skin. The wagon hit a bump, jolting us, and Ma winced, her eyes fluttering open.

"Are you ill, Ma?" I asked. I got to my knees, papers in hand, and crawled closer to her.

"No, Catherine."

"You're looking awful pale."

"I'm feeling what other women in my condition are feeling. Uncomfortable from this ride."

"If we could have waited until spring," I said. "Then you'd have had this baby while we were still in our house in Nauvoo. And no one would have been so cold."

"True. But others would have been with child on the move. And perhaps we would be too hot then."

"Maybe," I said, and thought about it a moment. Then, "Ma, what are some of your favorite things about Brother Joseph?"

"My favorite things?"

"Yes, ma'am. That you learned from him."

I could tell Ma was thinking. I watched her sway with the movement of the wagon.

"I'll tell you what I liked about the Prophet." Ma took a deep breath. "News came to us by word of mouth or in the *Morning and Evening Star*. I remember hearing his words about honoring the priesthood and the family."

Outside the rain fell harder. "And how he bore his imprisonment in Liberty Jail. He'd been there so long."

Ma stared off, remembering years back. "He was always so patient. Time and again he'd be cast away from us for months. Often the mobs would ridicule him or beat him. I always wondered how he could do it. I read his words later and set them forever in my heart." Ma found the page she was talking about. In a low voice, so that I almost didn't hear, she started speaking: "'The ends of the earth shall inquire after thy name,' Brother Joseph recorded..." Ma's tone made the air seem not so cold. I closed my eyes and listened. "'All these things shall give thee experience, and shall be for thy good.'"

What did God mean by that? That Brother Joseph was better because of the trials he went through? It seemed to make a bit of sense to me.

"I recall when he came back from jail after this. He spoke often of the hardships we would have to pass through. But he said we were the Saints of God," Ma said. "And I knew, by the way the Spirit touched my heart, that the things he said were true. He thought the Saints of God could do anything if they made an effort."

I still remembered Joseph Smith. It was less than two years since he had been murdered.

There were times when he came to where children were playing and joined in. He won every stick pull* contest I ever saw him play. He was strong.

And I remembered the day they brought him

and Brother Hyrum back from Carthage Jail, after they had been shot. It was awful. I didn't think I'd ever feel quite right again.

"I've told you why I joined the Church, haven't I, Catherine?" Ma asked.

"Yes, Ma," I said. "But tell me again. It'll help pass the time."

Pa looked back through the front opening to Ma and me. "It won't be much longer, Olive."

"Thank you, Michael." Ma's voice was soft. "We're fine back here."

A looked passed across Pa's face. It was one I had seen many times. Without any words coming from my pa's mouth, I could see how much he loved my ma. It warmed me through.

Pa turned forward.

"I was ten years old when Brother Joseph first saw God the Father and Jesus Christ. I lived only a few houses from him, and the story was told around our little community." I settled back and listened to the story of how Ma found the truth until, at last, our wagon pulled into camp.

CHAPTER FIVE

Brigham Young

There were people already at Sugar Creek when we got there. Men were making fires, women were starting dinner. I saw children gathering wood.

Pa pulled into a vacant area near everyone else. He helped Ma and me down from the wagon. Ma had a hard time moving, she'd sat so cramped. At last she limbered up, stretching herself this way and that.

"All loosened?" Pa asked.

"I am," Ma said, and then she set about making dinner for Pa and me. I looked for wood to keep our fire going and Pa took care of the animals.

It was bitter cold. My nose dripped and my

hands were freezing. I couldn't help wondering where the three of us would sleep tonight. Some people were making beds under their wagons. But the wind was biting. How would they be able to sleep the night through? A few were putting up tents. Others must be staying in their wagons. *I hope that's what we do,* I thought. I didn't like the idea of sleeping on the ground.

I gathered wood and made my way back to Ma and Pa. Aunt Millie was at our fire, which was small but growing.

"Nine?" Ma was saying. "In weather like this?"

"I can't believe it myself," Aunt Millie said. "But it's true."

I dropped the wood in a pile. Ma motioned me over to her with her fingertips.

"Nine babies were born the first night of camp. Right here," she said, pointing to the area around us.

"Here?" I asked. My voice went up high and squeaky.

"I don't think it'll be too much longer for me," Ma said. "I think this baby will be making its way into the world soon."

"What do you mean, Ma?"

Aunt Millie *tsk*ed. "Some things aren't meant to be talked about. The baby's coming, that's all to be told."

"I'm feeling it won't be too much longer," Ma said, looking straight at me, as if Aunt Millie hadn't even spoken.

"Well, Olive, I'll be around if you need me." Aunt Millie gave a sniff. I couldn't tell if it was because of the cold or because of me. "Send Michael over when the time arrives."

Ma nodded. "I will, Millie. Thank you so much for being here."

Aunt Millie walked toward her own wagon.

"Catherine," Ma said, "I'll need you be a brave girl when the birthing time comes."

"Ma," I said. "How can you do it out here?"

Ma looked around. The rain had stopped for the time being, but clouds were covering the night sky, blocking out the light of the stars. "It can be done," she said. "Nine babies were born before we even stepped foot here."

"It's so cold, though." I came close to Ma. She

held out one arm to me. I went into the shelter of it. And there I waited with her.

Where was Pa? Ma's face didn't look right in the firelight. I'd been with her when we'd eaten at a campfire before. Her face had never seemed this pale.

Maybe it was the cold.

I thought again of where we might sleep. The wagon was too full, and too narrow really, for the three of us to lie down in it.

I watched people coming into camp and setting up, also. It seemed wagons were rolling in every few minutes. How big would this camp get?

"I moved a log over closer to our fire," Ma said, "so we could warm up and not have to sit on the ground. It's so snowy there's no other place to sit. Unless we get out that tiny stool from when you were a little girl. The one Pa made you. Do you think you could still sit on that, Catherine?" Ma was smiling big at me, but she seemed tired.

"Probably a part of me could, Ma."

She laughed a bit. "Let's get as close as we can to the fire."

We moved over to the log and sat down. By

now the fire was a good-sized one. Ma's kettle sat off to the side, so the food wouldn't cook too quickly. Potato soup smell rose from the large, blackened pot.

"Where's Pa?"

"He *was* shoveling snow from under the wagon. Now I'm not sure where he is. But he'll be along directly, I'm sure."

A little uncomfortable feeling scooted into my stomach, and it wasn't one that meant I was hungry, either.

"Why would he shovel snow from under the wagon, Ma?"

"We'll need a place to sleep."

"But under the wagon?"

"Where else, Catherine?"

I shrugged my shoulders. "*Inside* maybe, Ma. It's so cold out here. How will we stay warm?" The unhappy feeling was back. Why would Ma and Pa be following anyone out of Nauvoo in weather like this?

In the distance I noticed a man wandering

from campfire to campfire. When I really paid attention to him, I saw him doing something at some of the cooking kettles.

It was dark except for the fires. These cast shadows on the canvas covers of the wagons nearby.

My face was warm, but my back was freezing. I turned around on the log and looked into the woods beyond.

"We should have stayed, Ma," I said. I couldn't say it looking her in the eye, but I could if I was warming my frozen back. Now, though, my face was being rained on. Tiny drops of ice fell onto my skin.

Ma didn't answer me. Instead she stood.

"Hello," said a voice.

I looked back behind me now. The man was at *our* camp. Had he come for food? Why hadn't he brought his own?

The firelight flickered onto the man's face. I realized that this was no beggar.

"Brother Brigham," Ma said.

"Is all well?" he asked. "It looks as if you've got a good fire going."

Ma nodded. "Michael made one as soon we pulled in here."

"I've been checking to see if everyone knows how to cook over an open flame like this."

"We're doing fine. I've had experience cooking out-of-doors before."

I should say, I thought. *Didn't we come in from Kirtland? Hadn't Ma been following Joseph Smith since he was fourteen years old? Now weren't both she and Pa following Brigham Young?*

"I've been helping the women who don't know how to cook outside. These aren't the best conditions tonight," he said.

"Shall I help too?" Ma asked. "I could go from camp to camp . . ."

Brigham Young looked at Ma, then smiled. "No, Sister. You stay here and keep your fire going. The Brethren and I will continue to watch over our little Camp of Israel."

He tipped his hat at Ma.

"We'll help any way we can," Ma said to him. "My husband will be back soon. If you need anyone who is used to this weather, call on him.

Catherine and I will be able to spare him if a need arises."

My head nearly jerked off my neck, I turned to look at Ma so fast.

Again he tipped his hat to Ma. "Thank you. The Lord will bless you mightily." He started away, then turned back to us. "There will be music and singing after the evening meals." Brigham Young left.

"Ma," I said, my voice breathy from being so surprised at what she had said. "How could you say that?"

"Say what, Catherine?" Ma was up now stirring the soup.

I turned back to face the fire and warm my front half. "How could say you'd let Pa go help other people? We need him here. *You* need him here."

Ma looked back at me. Her face was dark. She sat near me on the log. When she was close and the firelight was shining on her face, I could tell that this was not going to be a pleasant conversation.

Ma didn't get angry with me often. She and

Pa always let me speak my mind. Lots of other families believed that children should sit quiet. Not Ma and Pa. They wanted me to tell them how I felt about things. But I could tell by looking at Ma's face I had said the wrong thing.

"I will always serve the Lord, Catherine. In life and in death."

And with that she threw a small log on the fire.

CHAPTER SIX

Almost Time

Pa got back to us not long after that.

"Michael," Ma said. "It's time to eat."

"So my stomach has been telling me," Pa said. He leaned forward and kissed Ma's cheek. "Olive, your face is as cold as mine."

Ma smiled, but her smile was small. "It's nearly time."

Pa looked at her for a moment.

Ma handed him some soup. Steam rose from the cream-colored bowl, part of Ma's fine china that she had been carting around from place to place for years.

"Time for a blessing on the food?" he asked.

Ma shook her head. "Time for the baby."

"What?" Pa's voice was a shout. He leapt close to Ma, his potato soup sloshing as he went.

"Not quite yet," Ma said. And then she laughed. "I'm going to wash beans for tomorrow and set them to soak." Ma looked around, then mumbled, "I hope they don't freeze. Afterwards . . ."

"Whatever there is to be done," Pa said, "Catherine and I will do it, Olive. I want you to just rest. Today has been exhausting."

"I can't leave everything for you two. There's too much to be done. We all have . . ."

Pa interrupted Ma again. He took hold of her arm and, moving close to her face, said, "This isn't a good place to have a baby, Olive. I want you to take care. I want you to be as rested as you can."

A bit of fear started to fill up in my stomach.

Ma looked at Pa. At first I thought she might argue with him. Then she smiled. "Of course, you're right, Michael. I'll tell you both what to do. I'll be queen for the night. My throne will be the log."

I laughed then, feeling relieved.

Pa looked at me. "Eat quickly, Catherine. I want you to go and tell Aunt Millie the time is near."

After the blessing was said, I gulped my food, burning my mouth and almost not tasting the hot soup.

"Can you believe that another life will be coming to our home?" Ma said. Her face seemed to wiggle in the wavering light of the fire. "I have waited for so long. This is good. All will be well. I know it."

Even though I was still hungry, I set down my bowl and went looking for Aunt Millie. In the distance I heard Pitt's Band* starting up. Brigham Young was right. There would be music and dancing.

A few voices, laughing, drifted toward me.

Aunt Millie wasn't at her wagon. Neither was Uncle Ford.

They've gone dancing, I thought. *I'll go find them there.*

By now a lively dance tune was being played. I could hear someone laughing loud. When I got to the group, I saw Aunt Millie. She was shaking her head, and Uncle Ford was trying to pull her to the center of the ring of people.

"Ford," said Aunt Millie. "It's one thing to dance in a barn. It's another to dance in the cold outdoors."

"You have always been the best there is at dancing," Uncle Ford said. "I want you to show our friends here that a little snow and cold wind can't slow you down none."

People laughed, and a few women called "Millicent, dance for us."

In the firelight, Aunt Millie looked just like Ma. Exactly like her, only older. *Why,* I thought, almost reluctantly, *I see how Ma is going to look in fifteen years.*

Aunt Millie saw me, then, standing in the circle. The smile left her face and she rushed toward where I was.

I opened my mouth to say something but never had a chance. Aunt Millie grabbed my hand and sent me almost spinning back to our wagon.

Ma was no longer resting on the log. Pa held

onto her. Aunt Millie rushed to her side. She was all business.

"Michael, I'll need a shelter for Olive to rest in."

"Don't put me in the wagon," Ma said. "I don't think there's time to unload it. I've waited too long before telling anyone."

Aunt Millie's voice was soothing. "All will be well, sister." She leaned her head close to Ma's, and my mother tried to smile.

"I'll put up a tent," Pa said. And with that he was gone.

"We'll need all the clean snow you can find, Catherine," Aunt Millie said.

"I don't want to leave," I said. "I want to stay with Ma."

"Hurry, child," Aunt Millie said. Her voice pushed at me.

And so I did.

I ran off with two milk buckets to a small open area where the snow was untouched, fresh and clean. I scooped up handfuls until both buckets were heaping. Then I ran the long way back to our wagon.

Already a pot was set near the fire.

"Dump the snow there," Pa said.

I did, glad for the warmth that came from the flames. My whole body felt like a piece of ice. How cold was it? Surely below freezing. Ma's beans would have frozen after all.

Pa was making a fire on the other side of the tent he had put up for Ma.

Sleet was falling again.

"This is no time to be having a baby," Aunt Millie said.

In the distance came the sound of laughter. Pitt's Band started playing again.

Ma was resting in the tent now. Aunt Millie bustled around her, hurrying this way and that, chattering the whole time. "Then Ford—you know what a kidder he is—Ford tried to make me dance in front of the whole group of them."

"You've always been good at dancing," Ma said. Her voice sounded strange. Different.

Aunt Millie went on talking. The band went on playing. I stood in the background, wanting to be close to my mother. I warmed myself at the fire, toasting first my front then my back.

Catherine's Remembrance

"It's raining on your ma," Aunt Millie called to me. "Get a pie pan and let's see if we can't keep her a bit drier."

I looked through the box of Ma's dishes for flat pans.

"Michael, I'm going to need help. Please see if a few women won't come to keep Olive dry."

Pa took off at a run.

"Bring all the pans you can, Catherine," Aunt Millie said.

I found four. Two pie pans and two bread pans. They reminded me of Ma's peach pie and her bread. I carried the tins* to Ma and Aunt Millie.

Ma's face scared me. I'd never seen such a look of pain before. I dropped to my knees on the frozen ground. "Ma, Ma!" I said.

"Catherine," she said. "All will be well."

"Move out of the way, child," Aunt Millie said. "Your ma needs air."

"Let her stay with me, Millicent," Ma said. "I want to talk to her."

For once Aunt Millie didn't *tsk* at Ma's suggestion.

Catherine's Remembrance

"Climb in here next to me," Ma said.

I crawled next to Ma. Thin light found its way in to us. I could just see the outline of her face. The air I breathed in and out was cold. I knew I'd have seen the mist of our breath if only there had been more light.

"Catherine, I don't ever think I've told you of the evening you were born, have I?" Ma asked.

"No, ma'am, not that I remember," I said. "Pa did a little, though." I put my arm across Ma's chest. She felt cold and thin.

"I want to tell you."

A few women gathered close outside Ma's makeshift* tent. I could hear them talking about the weather and how it was too bad Ma couldn't have waited a day more before leaving Nauvoo.

"Circle around the opening," Aunt Millie said. "Catch the drops as they fall. We don't want the mother nor the child to get wet."

"You were so tiny, Catherine. And the moment you were born, you began to holler," Ma said.

"She's not stopped that, has she, Olive?" It was Pa, standing close outside.

Ma smiled. "You were crying so. And how I wanted to hold you. My ma had helped you to come into the world, and she said to me, 'Olive, touch your baby.' I did, Catherine. I reached out and touched your little back. As soon as my fingers met your skin, you stopped crying."

"I stopped?" I asked.

"Yes," Ma said. "I laid my hand on your back and every cry from you stopped, just like that."

"Tell her the rest of that miracle," Aunt Millie said.

"I will," Ma said. But her voice quieted right then. She closed her eyes tight and squeezed my arm between her hands.

"What, Ma?" I said. "You're hurting me. What's wrong?"

"She's all right," Aunt Millie said, squatting down at the tent opening.

Ma took in a ragged breath.

"Ma?" I asked.

"I'm fine, Catherine. Let me finish my story, then I want you to run on to Aunt Millie's wagon. Or to listen to the music."

"I want to stay with you, Ma."

"You can't, Catherine. You have to go."
"But Ma . . ."
"Let me tell you the miracle, Catherine."
"Yes, Ma," I said, my voice a whisper.
"My hand was on your back, and you were still as the night. Then I moved my hand so they could take you and clean you up. As soon as I did, you began to cry again. 'She knows you, Olive,' my ma said. And I knew it to be true, Catherine. You and I would always be the best of friends."

"It's true, Ma," I said. And tears came up warm in my eyes. "It's true. You are my closest friend. I've always wanted to be exactly like you, Ma."

"Let me kiss you good-bye," Ma said.

I leaned my face over to her. She pressed her dry lips against my cheek.

"Come on, girl," Pa said.

"I'm coming, Pa," I said, but I leaned close to Ma. I had to find something out from her. I had to know how she knew. "Ma," I whispered in her ear. "Ma, how do you know that this is what God wants from us? How do you know this is his true church?"

Ma looked at me, her eyes large in the darkness. "The Spirit has let me know."

"Let's go, Catherine," Pa said again.

"How do you know it's the Spirit and just not you making yourself feel that way?"

Ma took my hand tight in hers. "I know because my heart tells me. This perfect feeling of right is inside. Like I knew when Joseph Smith told of the gold plates. Like I knew that we would be best friends forever. This little voice inside me said, 'That's right.' It's different for everyone, Catherine. You'll find it. You'll know when the Spirit blesses you with understanding."

"I'll try, Ma," I said. "I'll try real hard."

Pa poked his head in at the tent bottom where the women were standing with pans, catching the freezing rain.

"Let's go," he said.

"I don't want to. I want to stay here with Ma." A feeling of panic set inside of me. I had to stay with Ma. I had to.

Pa reached one hand in. He moved his fingers to let me know I should follow him.

"Ma," I said. "Ma. I'm afraid to go. I'm afraid to leave you."

"All will be well, Catherine," she said.

"No, Ma," I said, and then I hugged her like I never had before.

"Catherine." Pa's voice was soft.

"Don't make me go, Pa," I said.

"It's time," Pa said.

I crawled out of the tent and looked back at my mother.

"I love you, Catherine," she said.

For a brief moment, a warm feeling rested in my heart.

"I love you too, Ma."

Then I went off to wait for her in Aunt Millie's wagon.

CHAPTER SEVEN

Learning for Myself

The wagon felt cold. It was cramped with more things than even our wagon held. And I couldn't sleep. I needed to know Ma was lying right there beside me, like a few minutes before. I needed to know that Pa was on the other side of the tent, listening to Ma talk to me.

I thought about Nauvoo. It would be so nice to be back there now.

No, wait. I sat up. "I will not think like that," I said out loud, even though there was no one near. "I'm going to try like Ma says I should. I have to think the right things before I can believe."

We were gone from Nauvoo because of greedy people. They didn't want Mormons in Illinois.

"Give us until spring," Brigham Young had said to the governor of the state. "Promise us fair sales on our homes and our city."

I knew from listening at meetings and at the dinner table that promises had been made. And that those same promises were broken. That's why we had crossed the Mississippi in the winter.

"We were run out of Nauvoo," I whispered in the dark. "I've known that the whole time."

And then it was clear to me. I was angry to be leaving, but Brigham Young wasn't forcing us anywhere. Mobs were. Like they had forced Joseph Smith from New York and then from town to town in Ohio and finally to Illinois, where they had eventually killed him.

I thought about Ma's words. "I'd waited so long, Catherine. I waited for the truth so long, and when young Joseph's story spread around the neighborhood, I knew it to be true. Then I waited for years for the restoration of the Church. At last it happened and I was baptized."

"How, Ma? How did you know it was right? How did you know it was true?"

"It says how to know for yourself in the last part of the book of Moroni," Ma had said.

That's what I needed to do, I decided in Aunt Millie's wagon. I knew she had a Book of Mormon. Where was it? I searched for a copy of the book. At last I found one, under the pillow she sat on to travel.

I leafed through the last few pages until I found the part Ma had spoken about. It was quiet out now, with only the sounds of people heading off to sleep after the dancing. I heard a baby cry and then a dog barked.

A bit of light came from a fire nearby. Wrapping a blanket around my shoulders, I aimed myself in such a way that the firelight flickered on the pages I wanted to study.

In the cold of that bitter night, I read about God's mercy to his children. I read about how the Holy Ghost can help people to know the truth of all things.

"All things," I said to myself. "I can know the truth about *all* things." I looked out at the flames of the nearby fire and the quieting camp.

Then I closed my eyes. "Heavenly Father," I

said. "I want to know if this is right for me like my ma knows. Are these things true?"

I waited. I didn't feel anything burning inside. I was a little worried about Ma. And a lot cold. But there was no answer.

Ma's voice came into my mind: "All will be well, Catherine."

I closed the book and lay back down. At last I went to sleep.

I woke before morning though I wasn't sure why. Except for the sound of the rain, the camp was still. Had I been dreaming of the Book of Mormon, I wondered?

I thought of Ma. A peaceful feeling filled up my heart. It was such a big feeling that I had to gasp to take in a breath. It was there only a minute.

"It's true," I said, to the dark. "Ma and Pa are right." Shivers covered my arms and legs.

Pa's voice reached into Aunt Millie's wagon, making me jump.

"Catherine?"

"Yes, Pa, I'm here."

"Come out to me, girl."

"Yes, sir," I said. I moved as quick as I could through Aunt Millie's things. I stuck my head through the flap in the back. Far away the sky began to lighten for morning, though it wasn't quite sunrise. My feeling warmed me like I knew the sun could.

Pa looked at me.

"Is the baby here?" I asked, because his face didn't seem right.

"She is," Pa said.

"A girl," I said, my voice riding out on the cold morning air.

Pa nodded. He looked down at the ground, then up at me in the wagon.

The feeling of peace came back, full and strong.

"Oh, Pa," I said. And then somehow I knew. I struggled to get out of the wagon. "Oh, Pa."

"Your ma didn't make it," Pa said. Rain pelted him. It dripped from his hat, spattered hard on his shoulders, and ran in tiny streams down his jacket.

"Pa," I said, because it was all I *could* say.

"Your ma didn't make it," he said again, wiping at his face with the flat of his big hand.

Even though I knew, I didn't want to hear what he was saying.

"Is the baby here?" I asked again.

Pa nodded.

"Can I see Ma?"

Pa looked at me funny for a moment.

"Your ma is dead," he said.

"I know."

Pa kept talking. "Your ma died. The baby is here, and your ma is gone." He started to cry, then held out his arms to me. I couldn't ever remember my pa crying. Not ever.

The peaceful feeling was there, so real I felt I could touch it if I wanted to. I didn't think I could move, though, not even an inch.

"Come to me, Catherine," Pa said, his voice cracking with sorrow.

Somehow, then, I crawled out into the freezing rain to Pa. For the first time in a long time, he picked me up like I was a tiny girl and cradled me in his arms. He stood there, quiet, only his breath making sounds. Then he sucked in the cold night air, and his crying stopped.

Pa started back, carrying me to where we had camped. His steps were sure in the muddy earth. In the distance, over his shoulder, I saw the sky lighting up—a thin, gray line, cold like everything around us. Pa held my face close up to his, and his hat kept the rain from splattering on my skin that was icy with the thought of my ma being gone.

Slowly the warmth of my feeling left me.

"Ma," I cried out, and a horse nickered in the distance.

"Shhh," Pa said. "It'll be hard, but we can do it." His voice was soft. His beard rubbed against my neck.

"Oh, Ma."

Pa stood in the rain outside our wagon and let me cry. On the ground was the tent. I could see that she was still there. I heard Aunt Millie inside the tent, talking low to Ma.

"All will be well now, Olive," I heard her say. My aunt began to cry.

Catherine's Remembrance

After a bit, Pa set me down on my feet, but he kept his hand strong on my shoulder.

"The baby's in the wagon," Pa said. I could hear the sadness thick in his voice. "One of the women who lost her own child is taking care of her."

I turned back to the tent. "I want my ma," I said. And then I was crying.

Pa reached out and grabbed me to him. "Hush," he said.

"I want my ma," I said. "I want to tell her good-bye."

I pulled away from Pa and stumbled over the cold ground to the tent, but Pa caught hold of me again.

"Ma!" I called out.

Aunt Millie came out of the tent. In the early morning I could see that she had been crying, though there was no trace of tears.

"Don't stand in the rain and cry, Catherine," she said to me, her voice sad. "You're not the first to lose her mother, and sure as there is a God, you won't be the last. Now pick up your chin and don't waste another tear at what can't be changed."

Pa stood quiet and Aunt Millie turned to him.

"Michael, keep the baby warm and I think that she'll be all right," Aunt Millie said. Then her voice cracked wide open, showing me the sorrow she felt. She stood still, biting on her bottom lip, then walked over to me. Her hand reached out and touched my face.

In a voice like Ma's, Aunt Millie said, "Mourn in private, child. Tears aren't for the world but between you and God our Father."

Aunt Millie looked at Pa. "I'll tell Brother Brigham," she said, and left.

The sun crept up, turning the camp an orange color.

I looked at the tent. More tears came into my eyes, but the warm feeling was there again.

"All will be well, Catherine." Ma's last words to me came back true. I climbed into the wagon.

"Would you like to hold her?" the woman asked me.

I shook my head. "No. I don't think so."

The baby let out a small *mew* sound. I moved closer so I could see her.

"She's beautiful," the woman said.

I didn't think so, but I didn't say anything. Her face was wrinkled and her nosed looked mashed.

"She has a strong cry."

"So did I, my ma says," I said.

"I know. Your ma told me about you. When little Camilla was born, your ma reached to touch her, to quiet her cries."

I leaned close to the woman now, my breath caught in my throat. "And what happened?" I asked.

"The baby quieted right down," the woman said. "I've not seen that happen before. As soon as your ma touched the baby, the crying stopped."

For a moment I couldn't do anything but think. *She's like I was,* I thought. *This baby was like me.*

"I'd like to hold her now," I said.

The woman handed Camilla to me, then made her way out of the wagon. Outside I heard her talking to Pa. "Bring the baby down, Brother Michael. I will feed her for you."

"Thank you," Pa said. And his voice was soft.

CHAPTER EIGHT

My Own Remembrance

Pa climbed up into the wagon.

"She's not so pretty," I said.

"All new babies look like that," Pa said. His lips were turned down in a frown. I could see he was trying to be brave. I was trying too. Tears sat in my eyes.

"She's too red and wrinkled. She doesn't look a thing like Sister Smith's baby. Her baby was much bigger."

"Well, her baby was older when you saw it that first time."

Outside, the camp was starting to come to life. How many of them knew my ma was dead? I wondered. A hard lump came up in my throat.

"That lady told me Ma touched this baby..." I couldn't go on. I was feeling too sad.

"Camilla?" Pa asked, though she was the only baby he and I knew.

I nodded. "She said Ma touched Camilla when she was brand-new and crying, and the baby stopped fussing." I was whispering now.

"It's true," Pa said. "I was listening. I heard it."

I looked again at the baby. Maybe she wasn't so bad. "Do you know what that means?" I asked Camilla. She opened one eye, then closed it. "It means that you and Ma will be best friends forever," I said. "Like she and I are."

And then I started crying.

After we buried Ma, Pa called me into the wagon.

"What is it, Pa?"

"Your ma wanted you to have this," he said. He dug under the seat and pulled out Ma's remembrance box and handed it to me.

"The things in there were what helped her to remember good times," he said. "I'll leave you alone to look through it."

"Thanks, Pa," I said.

Outside, the wind whistled as it blew past the wagons. Brigham Young had decided that we would stay camped here awhile. Baby Camilla was with Sister Carolyn being fed. Aunt Millie would be taking the baby for awhile, until her next feeding. Then Pa and I would take care of her.

It was cold in the wagon, but colder outside, so I sat near where Ma had rested the day we traveled to Sugar Creek. I could smell Ma in the blankets. It made me feel awful lonely for her.

Ma's remembrance box opened with a squeak. I took the things out of it, one at a time.

On top were two of my favorite rocks, the gold piece and the geode that Uncle Ford had given me.

"When did she get these from my collection?" I asked. "Oh, Ma, how sweet of you."

I'd never thought to bring a bit of what was important. I'd only thought to want it all.

There was a gold chain, the clasp broken. What had that

meant to Ma? Who could tell me? Maybe Pa, or even Aunt Millie.

There was a bit of hair, curly and dark, tied with a pale green ribbon.

"Why, this is probably a lock of my own hair," I said.

Finally there was a packet of letters, also tied with a ribbon. Were these letters written to Ma from Pa? Did Ma intend for me to read her courtship notes? I knew Ma and Pa loved one another. They were always touching, sharing gentle looks. Would I be able to tell how they felt by reading these things? Should I even read their private thoughts?

"Ma gave these to you, Catherine," I said to myself. I slipped the ribbon from the small sheaf of letters. "'May 20, 1834,'" I read. "'My Dear Catherine...'"

"This is to me," I said aloud. A letter from my mother.

I started reading again.

Catherine's Remembrance

My Dear Catherine,

You are only just born but I have sent your pa to Mother's house for ink because we are out. I want to express these feelings that I am sure I will never forget, but that I need to capture while they are fresh.

How dear you are to me. As I hold you close, Little One, I realize the teachings of Brother Joseph are most true. We are indeed created after the image of God. I see it this day in your perfect-ness.

I stopped reading.

"Oh, Ma," I said, tears falling down my cheeks. "Oh, Ma. What will I ever do without you?"

I clutched the letters to my heart and cried. My hands were shaking, and the tears were coming so fast I was sure I'd not be able to read what Ma had written. I thumbed through a few letters, moving to the last in the pile.

Feb. 16, 1846

My Dearest Catherine,

I have looked over these letters to you, before sitting down to pen a few lines. We leave beloved Nauvoo today.

Catherine's Remembrance

I am surprised at how shallow my love was for you at your birth. I didn't realize, then, how strongly I could love you. Your father, only, is closer to me than you are.

I am excited to be able to share this love with the baby we will soon have. I look forward to the time I can hold this child in my arms.

My tears started to fall again. Ma hadn't even had the chance to hold Camilla. The thought nearly broke my heart in two.

I know you will be an excellent sister, just as you have been an excellent daughter. Won't we all be wonderful friends?
Seek to know truth. You will find it.
Eternally in God's Kingdom,
Your Loving Mother

"How long will I miss you?" I cried out.

Suddenly I remembered the feeling I had had in Aunt Millie's wagon.

This feeling was from God. I knew it. I don't know how I knew it, but I did. The remembrance of this feeling would give me strength when I missed Ma. It was a comfort to me from Him.

"Oh, Ma," I said. "You were right."

After awhile I gathered Ma's remembrances back into her box. I slid it back into the place Pa had put it to keep it safe when we began our trip. Had that only been a few days ago? It seemed a forever.

I took a deep breath and, gathering what courage I could from my own remembrance, went to find Camilla. She was with Aunt Millie, fussing.

"Let me try holding her," I said.

Aunt Millie *tsk*ed. Then she looked at me. "I guess I should let you care for her awhile. I can get something cooking for dinner if you do."

I took Camilla, tiny in her bundle, back to our wagon. Pa was at a meeting that Brigham Young was holding.

I made careful steps along the snowy ground. Once I was home, I laid Camilla in the back of the wagon, then climbed up next to her. By the time I had settled us both in Ma's spot, the baby was almost asleep. And I wasn't feeling quite so lonely.

"I hope you can hear me," I said to my sister. "I have to tell you a story about a good friend of mine. And of yours, too. I want to tell you about our ma."

GLOSSARY
In Catherine's Own Words

buttonhook—A metal hook that helped me button my shoes. The buttons on my shoe were small and hard to get through the holes. The buttonhook helped me pull the button into the hole. See page 22.

clicked to the oxen—To get the oxen moving, we make a clicking sound. Somehow, the animals seem to know that it means, "Get going!" See page 34.

clothes press—A large, tall cabinet that holds a person's clothes. See page 10.

family way—To be polite, people said a woman was *in the family way* when she was going to have a baby. See page 3.

friv'lous—When Pa told me take nothing *friv'lous*, he was telling me there was no space on the wagon for anything that couldn't be used later. You don't spell the word quite the way I said it. It's spelled *frivolous*. See page 3.

geode—A stone that from the outside looks like a plain, round rock. But it has a secret cavity inside, lined with beautiful crystals. See page 11.

Glossary

lashed down—If the wagons weren't lashed down on the barges, they would have rolled right off and into the icy Mississippi. Lashing a wagon was much more secure than just tying it. The wheels were kept from rolling by putting them in the locked position and usually something was jammed through the wheels in the back so they wouldn't be able to move. See page 30.

looking glass—A mirror. See page 22.

makeshift—Temporary or a substitute for the real thing. The makeshift tent was something that was thrown together to cover Ma. It wasn't an official tent, just something to try and keep the snow off her. See page 59.

Nauvoo Police—A band of men that helped to protect the Mormons. I feel safer when I know they're keeping an eye on things. See page 27.

newsprint—A page from the newspaper. See page 39.

on the morrow—An fancier way of saying *tomorrow*. See page 8.

Pitt's Band—We all enjoyed hearing Pitt's Band, one of the most well known in Nauvoo, when they played their lively tunes. See page 55.

poultice—To make a poultice, Ma heated an ointment of some kind, often homemade, and spread it on the chest and neck of the sick person. Then she covered the ointment with a clean, dry cloth. See page 18.

Glossary

riding board—If you were going to ride on a wagon, you sat on the *riding board*—not for comfort, because it was not a comfortable seat, but more because you were guiding the oxen or because you were too young, too sick, too tired, or too old to walk. See page 25.

running on—When Pa asked Ma if I was *running on,* he meant was I still talking. See page 1.

slips—Brother Brigham Young wanted us to take anything we could to our new place of safety. In Nauvoo we cut *slips of fruit trees,* branches that would grow to be trees when we planted them once we got to where we were going. See page 11.

stick pull—A game that showed a person's strength. Brother Joseph was the best. I've heard it told he was never beaten. Two people would sit opposite each other with a stick between them. At the word, both would begin to pull, each hoping to be able to lift the other person from the ground and over to his own side. See page 41.

tethered—The animals were *tethered,* or tied, tightly to the boat so they wouldn't plunge into the water. See page 28.

tins—Another name for bread or pie pans. See page 58.

wagon cover—An arched canvas cloth cover, held up with curved wooden or metal bands, made a kind of tent over the top of the wooden wagon bed. This provided some protection for the contents of the wagon, and a person could

GLOSSARY

sit under the wagon cover for some protection from wind, rain, and snow. See page 38.

yoked together—Draft animals such as oxen worked in teams of two, and we kept them both headed in the same direction by attaching a yoke—a heavy wooden framework—that held both of them loosely around their necks. See page 29.

What Really Happened

Brigham Young had been studying a way to get the Saints to a safe place for some time before he made the call for the people of Nauvoo to move. He had plans that each person should have a year's supply of food on board their wagons. He wanted his people to be prepared. The Mormons weren't planning to leave Illinois, though, until warm weather. Those anxious to get the Saints out of Nauvoo began to raise their voices in threatenings. Brigham Young held on as long as he could before letting everyone know that it would be safer to face the elements than to stay in their homes in Nauvoo.

On February 4, 1846, the first group of people began to make their way across the Mississippi River. What happened to Catherine and her family is what happened to many people as they tried to cross the huge, icy river.

What Really Happened

Eventually, the river froze solid enough that wagons drove across on the ice.

The first night, in the first camp, named Sugar Creek, nine babies were born. During the next few months, as the first groups of Saints were leaving Nauvoo, a great deal happened in a very short time, and much of it was very interesting.

Catherine and her family are imaginary. But the historical events of this story really took place, and the details of life during the Nauvoo exodus are as accurate as I can make them.

About the Author

No wonder Carol Lynch Williams enjoys writing books for girls—she's surrounded by them! After having grown up with a sister and her grandmother, Carol married and had four daughters of her own. She is expecting a fifth baby.

Carol grew up in Florida and joined the LDS Church when she was seventeen. She served a full-time LDS mission to deaf people in North Carolina and then moved to Utah, where she attended BYU, worked as an interpreter for the deaf, and began writing books. She and her family live in Mapleton, Utah. Carol teaches Relief Society and is Achievement Day leader in her ward Primary.

Carol's husband, Drew, writes, "Carol fills her family's life with her youthful sense of humor, great story telling, and the yummiest bread a mom can bake!"

Carol has written five nationally published novels and five LDS novels. Earlier Latter-day Daughters books include *Sarah's Quest, Anna's Gift, Esther's Celebration, Marciea's Melody,* and *Laurel's Flight.*

From *Hannah's Treasure*
Another Exciting New Title
in the Latter-day Daughters Series

Poppy steered us closer to the swarm of people on the Philadelphia street corner. I noticed right off that plenty of the folks here looked like farmers. The fine-dressed people didn't look interested.

"Some kind of preacher, I reckon," Poppy said, stepping nearer. "Let's hold up and see what he has to say." We Ellisons have always been respectful of preachers.

As we wiggled in further, I thought I'd heard the voice before. Poppy must have felt something too, 'cause he stopped and tilted his head like our dogs Harley and Farish do when they're listening hard. I was more taken with the look on Poppy's face than anything the preacher was saying.

Poppy said, "That's *him*," like he was talking to himself.

"Who?" I asked. But he didn't hear me. Something this man was talking about had sure caught a grip on my pa. He stood looking like there was a spell come over him. 'Cept we don't believe in spells.